STEVE
THE MULE

To Scott and Jessie for all your brilliant ideas
and
To Cissie for inspiring Steve the Mule

Special thanks to Rob for bringing Steve the Mule to life.
Your talents are awe-inspiring!

Text copyright © 2017 by Shanna Hatfield.
Illustrations copyright © 2017 by Rob Foote.
All rights reserved. Printed in the U.S.A.

ISBN: 978-0-9980988-2-1

No part of this publication may be reproduced, distributed, or transmitted in any form or by any means, including photocopying, recording, or other electronic or mechanical methods, without the prior written permission of the author, except in the case of brief quotations embodied in critical reviews and certain other noncommercial uses permitted by copyright law.

For permission requests, please contact the author, with a subject line of "permission request" at the email address below or through her website.
shanna@shannahatfield.com
shannahatfield.com

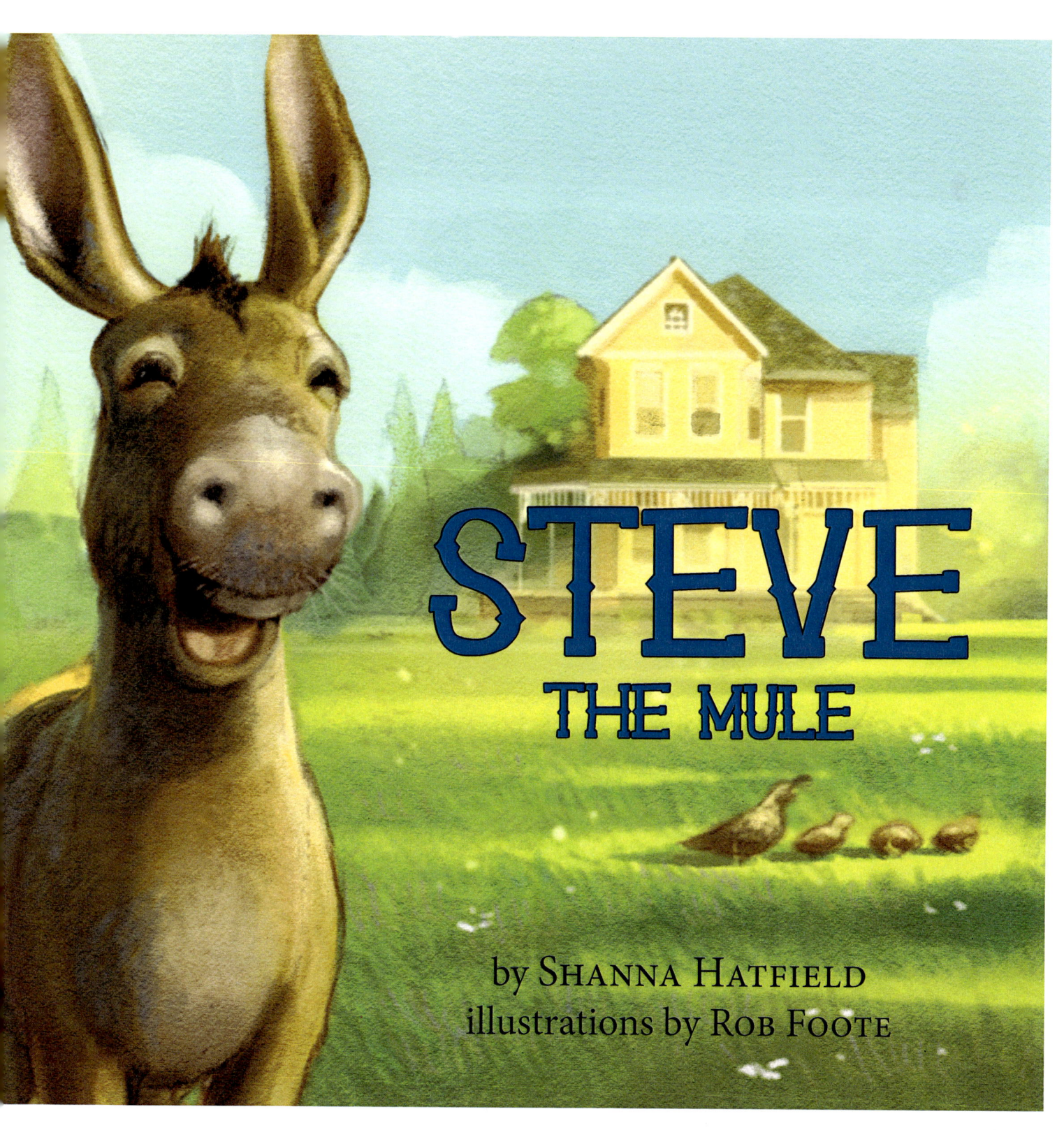

HOWDY!

Welcome to Pendleton and our farm.
I'm Steve —

                Steve the Mule.

Meet Riley, Bertie, and Willa. They are my family.

I've known Riley since he was knee-high to a grasshopper.
(That's pretty small, in case you're wondering.)

Riley and I rode on the train all the way across the prairie and over mountains to Pendleton where he fell in love with a beautiful girl.

I decided right away I liked Bertie. She loves Riley. She smells nice. And she scratches my chin.

I wasn't sure if I'd like Willa when she first arrived, but I got used to her.

I'd call her a pest,
 but she is kind of cute.

Even when she pulls my ears...

And away from the bulls...

And the chickens, but that's mostly for the benefit of the chickens.

They **squawk** when she grabs their tail feathers.

Bertie gets upset if Willa **wallows** with the pigs.

This is Mud, Riley's horse. It's okay for Willa to pet him. The other horses think she's a wild animal, especially if she *tugs* on their manes or tails.

Yep!
I take *good* care of Willa.

I settle beneath a shady tree and rest my eyes for a little while. Zzzz zzz...

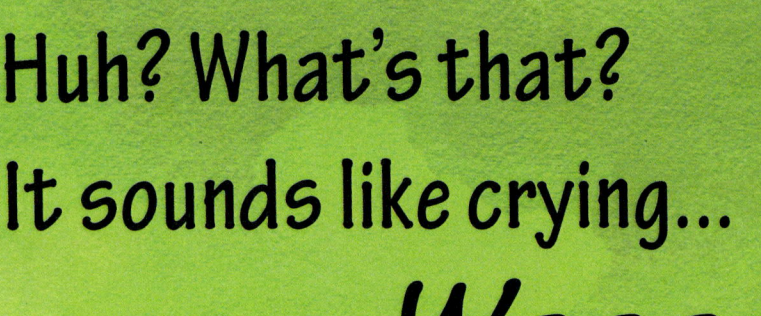

Huh? What's that?
It sounds like crying...
Waaaahhhhh!

Oh, no!
There's a sneaky ol' coyote trying to corner Willa!

It's a good thing
I'm on duty guarding
Willa and our farm.

Made in the USA
San Bernardino, CA
20 November 2017